Kamala Harris:
History-Making US Vice President

James Roland

ReferencePoint
Press®

San Diego, CA

About the Author

James Roland started out as a newspaper reporter more than twenty-five years ago and then moved on to become an editor, magazine writer, and author.

Picture Credits:
Cover: Naresh777/Shutterstock

6: Associated Press
11: Associated Press
14: Elijah Nouvelage/Reuters/Newscom
19: Kelvin Sterling Scott/iStock
22: Elijah Nouvelage/Reuters/Newscom
27: MATJAZ SLANIC/iStock

30: Associated Press
33: Featureflash Photo Agency/Shutterstock.com
37: Associated Press
40: Associated Press
42: Jose Ivan Cazares/Shutterstock.com
47: Associated Press
49: Aaron of L.A. Photography/Shutterstock
52: Pat Benic/UPI/Newscom

LIBRARY OF CONGRESS CATALOGING-IN-PUBLICATION DATA

Names: Roland, James, author.
Title: Kamala Harris: history-making US Vice President / by James Roland.
Description: San Diego, CA : ReferencePoint Press, 2022. | Includes
    bibliographical references and index.
Identifiers: LCCN 2021004381 (print) | LCCN 2021004382 (ebook) | ISBN
    9781678200862 (library binding) | ISBN 9781678200879 (ebook)
Subjects: LCSH: Harris, Kamala, 1964---Juvenile literature. |
    Vice-Presidents--United States--Biography--Juvenile literature. | Women
    legislators--United States--Biography--Juvenile literature. | African
    American women legislators--Biography--Juvenile literature.
Classification: LCC E901.1.H37 R65 2021 (print) | LCC E901.1.H37 (ebook)
    | DDC 973.934092 [B]--dc23
LC record available at https://lccn.loc.gov/2021004381
LC ebook record available at https://lccn.loc.gov/2021004382

CONTENTS

Introduction   4

The Groundbreaking Journey of Kamala Harris

Chapter One   8

A Daughter of Immigrants

Chapter Two   17

Harris Finds Her Voice

Chapter Three   25

A Rising Star

Chapter Four   35

Senator Harris

Chapter Five   44

The Remarkable Path to the White House

Source Notes   54
Important Events in the Life of Kamala Harris   58
For Further Research   60
Index   62

The Groundbreaking Journey of Kamala Harris

On a cold and breezy afternoon in Washington, DC, with the world watching and her family surrounding her, Kamala Devi Harris took the oath of office to become the forty-ninth vice president of the United States. It was January 20, 2021. She was elected two months earlier as the running mate of President Joe Biden—a history-making achievement for many reasons. A former Democratic senator from California, Harris became the first woman vice president, as well as the first Black vice president and the first vice president of South Asian descent. Harris's mother was born in India, and her father was born in Jamaica, making her also the first vice president born to two immigrants in the country's 240-plus-year history. As a graduate of Howard University in Washington, DC, she is also the first graduate of a historically Black college or university to reach the White House.

The string of firsts is even longer than this. Her 2003 election as San Francisco district attorney and her 2010 election as California attorney general marked the first time a woman had served in those roles. And her 2016 election as one of California's two US senators also made her the first African American woman to represent the state in the Senate and the first South Asian American ever to serve as a US senator.

In her first speech as vice president, Harris stood outside the Lincoln Memorial and reminded the nation that her accomplishments were a reflection of what is possible in the

United States when people follow their dreams with determined actions. With the Washington Monument rising into the night sky behind her, she said:

It is my honor to be here, to stand on the shoulders of those who came before, to speak tonight as your vice president. In many ways, this moment embodies our character as a nation. It demonstrates who we are, even in dark times. We not only dream, we do. We not only see what has been, we see what can be. We shoot for the moon and then we plant our flag on it. We are bold, fearless, and ambitious. We are undaunted in our belief that we shall overcome, that we will rise up.[1]

Early Influences

Harris's long list of achievements was set in motion at a young age. As a child of immigrant parents, Harris occasionally visited relatives on opposite sides of the globe, giving her an early glimpse of a larger world and lessons that do not appear in a textbook. In a speech to a group called South Asians for Biden on the 2020 campaign trail, Harris recalled visits to her mother's hometown of Madras (which was later renamed Chennai) in eastern India. "In Madras, I would go on long walks with my grandfather, who at that point was retired, and we'd take morning walks where I pulled his hand and he would tell me about the heroes who are responsible for the birth of the world's biggest democracy, and he would explain that 'It's on us to pick up where they left off.' Those lessons are a big reason why I am where I am today,"[2] Harris says.

Harris often credits her late mother, Shyamala Gopalan, with inspiring her to stand up for herself and dream big. On the morning of her inauguration, Harris tweeted a picture of herself when she was a baby being held by her mother, who died of cancer in 2009. It was accompanied by the words "Thinking of my mother today. She was smart, fierce, and my first campaign staffer—and I dearly wish she were here with us for this moment. Her spirit still drives me to fight for our values."[3]

Though her parents divorced when she was young, they both had a profound influence on the future vice president. They marched and spoke out in the civil rights movement in the 1960s, making social justice a bedrock principle that guided Harris through her school years and her professional career. As vice president, Harris has pledged to focus much of her energy on issues such as criminal justice reform, environmental protection, racial justice, immigration reform, and ending economic inequality.

Over the years, Harris has impressed many people—including classmates, teachers, coworkers, and political opponents—with

With her hand on two Bibles held by her husband, Douglas Emhoff, Kamala Harris takes the oath of office as vice president.

her intelligence, toughness, and sense of humor. She is well known for her infectious laugh and beaming smile, as well as her desire to inspire others, especially young people. Her message to kids is very much like the one her mother passed on to her: do not let your crit-

ics hold you back from achieving your potential. Harris frequently directs that message to girls who may grow up as she did to enter professions where women, and especially women of color, are in the minority. In a 2019 interview in *Marie Claire*, Harris said:

> What I want young women and girls to know is: You are powerful and your voice matters. You're going to walk into many rooms in your life and career where you may be the only one who looks like you or who has had the experiences you've had. But you remember that when you are in those rooms, you are not alone. We are all in that room with you applauding you on. Cheering your voice. And just so proud of you. So you use that voice and be strong.[4]

CHAPTER ONE

A Daughter of Immigrants

Kamala Harris was born on October 20, 1964, in Oakland, California, and spent the next few years growing up in a little yellow duplex in nearby Berkeley. Her parents had come to the United States to complete their educations and launch their careers. In 1958 her mother, Shyamala Gopalan, graduated early from college in India. She was only nineteen. She then left to pursue a master's degree in nutrition and endocrinology at the University of California, Berkeley. The brilliant, ambitious teenager had never set foot in the United States before arriving there to begin the next chapter of her life. A few years later, Kamala's father, Donald Harris, left his homeland of Jamaica for Berkeley to get his PhD in economics. Tall and intensely curious, Harris had grown fascinated by labor and economics working part time in his grandmother's general store and talking with workers on his other grandmother's sugarcane farm in the summers.

Gopalan and Harris met in the fall of 1962, at a time when the civil rights movement was gaining momentum in the San Francisco Bay Area and other parts of the country. Both were attending a meeting of the recently formed Afro-American Association. Harris was speaking to other students about social and racial issues in Jamaica and comparing them to what he was seeing in the United States. Berkeley was fast becoming one of the centers of student activism, which was one of the reasons Harris wanted to continue his education there. When he was still in Jamaica, Harris read a news story about Berkeley student activists heading to the South to campaign for civil rights. "Further investigation of information about this university convinced me I had to go there,"[5] he said in a 2020 interview in the *New York Times*.

Impressed by his talk that fall afternoon, Gopalan went up to Harris after the meeting and started asking questions. "This was all very interesting to me, and I daresay, a bit charming," Harris recalled in the *New York Times* article. "At a subsequent meeting, we talked again, and at the one after that. The rest is now history."[6] The couple married in 1963, with Gopalan rejecting Indian culture's custom of arranged marriages and following her heart. A year later Kamala was born. In 1967 the couple had a second daughter, Maya, who grew up to be an accomplished lawyer like her older sister, as well as one of Kamala's top campaign advisers.

Early Exposure to Social Justice

Throughout much of the tumultuous 1960s, the couple participated in protests and rallies, confronting issues such as the racist apartheid government in South Africa and economic and racial injustice in the United States. And as the two marched with others down the tree-lined sidewalks of Berkeley, there was Kamala, too young to understand what all the activity was about but already hearing messages about social justice. At an August 2020 campaign appearance, Kamala Harris said:

> My parents would bring me to protests strapped tightly in my stroller. My mother, Shyamala, raised my sister, Maya, and me to believe that it was up to us and every generation of Americans to keep on marching. She'd tell us, "Don't sit around and complain about things; do something." So

9

I did something. I devoted my life to making real the words carved in the United States Supreme Court: Equal justice under law.[7]

The family moved for a brief period to the Midwest, first to Illinois in 1966 and then to Wisconsin. In Wisconsin, Harris and Gopalan took on teaching and research positions at the University of Wisconsin, Madison. But by then their marriage was in trouble. Gopalan decided to return to California in 1969 and take her daughters with her. Not long afterward, Harris became a professor of economics at Stanford University, less than 50 miles (80 km) south of Berkeley. In 1972 the couple divorced, and Gopalan retained full custody of the girls.

> "My mother, Shyamala, raised my sister, Maya, and me to believe that it was up to us and every generation of Americans to keep on marching."[7]
>
> —Kamala Harris

For a brief time after the custody battle, Harris saw little of his daughters. But as time went on, Kamala and Maya visited their father during summer vacations and other times through the years. He occasionally took the girls to visit his hometown in Jamaica and see the little store where he had helped his grandmother many years before. The girls explored the same hills and trails their father had hiked as a boy and got to know the wide, extended family that always welcomed them with open arms every time they returned to the island.

Kamala Goes to School

During this period of marital turbulence, Kamala reached the age when many kids start kindergarten. The year 1969 was also a time when the racial justice issues of the adult world were spilling over into the schools. Neighborhoods in many parts of the country, including Berkeley, were largely segregated, meaning that their schools were, too. Schools tended to be mostly White or mostly Black. With hopes of improving race relations and making cities and towns more integrated, school districts started busing programs that would send Black students into predominantly White schools and vice versa.

Kamala was a member of the second class to be integrated at her elementary school. To help fulfill the city's efforts to desegregate its elementary schools, Kamala and her classmates were bused across town to Thousand Oaks Elementary School. Each bus transporting kids across the city was labeled with a color and an animal. Harris rode "the red rooster" from her working-class neighborhood to the more affluent north Berkeley Hills area. "I only learned later that we were part of a national experiment in desegregation with working-class black children from the flatlands being bused in one direction and wealthier white children from the Berkeley hills bused in the other,"[8] Harris wrote in her 2019 memoirs, *The Truths We Hold: An American Journey*.

In 2004, Kamala Harris is sworn in as San Francisco's district attorney, as her mother, Shyamala Gopalan (center) looks on.

Though she had a longer bus ride than she would have had otherwise, she did not mind. She and her friends sang songs and played hand-clapping games. Harris looks back at her first few years of school fondly and holds a special teacher dear to her heart. In a 2019 interview with the Berkeleyside digital newspaper, Harris said:

> Growing up, the first question asked of me at the dinner table was, "What did you learn at school today?" Thanks to my beloved first-grade teacher, Mrs. Frances Wilson at Thousand Oaks Elementary School in Berkeley, I always had an answer I was anxious to share. Mrs. Wilson had a profound effect on all of us and was deeply committed to her students, a diverse group, ranging from kids growing up in housing projects to the children of people working at the university.[9]

Today there is a painted image of Kamala Harris on a playground wall at Thousand Oaks, alongside portraits of Malala Yousafzai, Serena Williams, and Anne Frank.

Race and Identity

Being raised by parents of different races and cultures meant Kamala grew up with a variety of influences. Her mother took the girls to a predominantly Black Baptist church, where Kamala sang in the youth choir, but also to a Hindu temple. In the day care they attended in the afternoons while Gopalan worked, Kamala and Maya were surrounded by posters of Rosa Parks, Harriet Tubman, and Sojourner Truth—three remarkable Black women from history. The day care sat on the first floor of an apartment building in Oakland. On the top floor was the apartment where Gopalan and her daughters moved after the divorce.

And in that new home, Kamala learned much about the Hindu faith and Indian culture and language from her mother. When Gopalan was frustrated with work or speaking affectionately to her daughters, the words were in Tamil, the language she grew up speaking. The words with the deepest emotions were spoken in

The Woman Whose Influence Mattered Most

Kamala Harris's career as a strong-willed leader willing to break barriers is a reflection of her mother. When Shyamala Gopalan graduated from college in the 1950s, she hoped to embark on a career in science but opportunities for women in that field were limited in India during those years. So Gopalan applied to the University of California, Berkeley. There she obtained advanced degrees in nutrition and endocrinology.

Although Gopalan was a petite woman—she was just 5 feet (152.4 cm) tall—Harris has always viewed her mother as a giant. Stories about Gopalan being denied a teaching job that was given to a less-qualified man and being mocked for her thick Indian accent resonated with Harris. During the August 2020 Democratic National Convention, Harris listed several famous women who had broken color and gender barriers in the past. And then she added, "There's another woman . . . whose shoulders I stand on. And that's my mother, Shyamala Gopalan Harris." Gopalan died of cancer in 2009, never getting to see Kamala become a senator or vice president. But others see Gopalan in Harris. Family friend Sharon McGaffie says Harris's achievements reflect Gopalan's determination and "that strength that she's fighting for something, that she's never intimidated."

Quoted in Rikha Sharma Rani, "The Woman Who Led Kamala Harris to This Moment," *The Atlantic*, October 25, 2020. www.theatlantic.com.

Quoted in Casey Tolan, "Kamala Harris: How Immigrants Shaped Her Life," *San Jose (CA) Mercury News*, February 10, 2019. www.mercurynews.com.

the language closest to Gopalan's heart. Growing up, Kamala often wore Indian jewelry and learned many Indian traditions. One in particular, the breaking of coconuts at a Hindu temple, is said to bring good luck. When Kamala was running for California attorney general in 2010, she called an aunt in India and asked her to smash coconuts at the temple Kamala had visited with her grandfather. Her aunt complied—and Kamala won that election. "All my friends were Black and we got together and cooked Indian food and painted henna on our hands, and I never felt uncomfortable with my cultural background,"[10] she says.

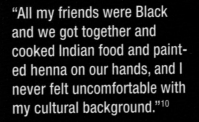

"All my friends were Black and we got together and cooked Indian food and painted henna on our hands, and I never felt uncomfortable with my cultural background."[10]

—Kamala Harris

Maya Harris (left), also a talented attorney, served as her older sister's campaign adviser as Harris pursued the nomination as the Democratic presidential candidate.

Although their mother was very proud of her Indian roots, it was clear from the time Kamala and Maya were young that society would view them as Black. "My mother understood very well she was raising two Black daughters," Harris wrote in her 2018 autobiography. "She knew that her adopted homeland would see Maya and me as Black girls, and she was determined to make sure we would grow into confident Black women."[11]

At times, Harris has opted to avoid questions or conversations about her multiracial identity and what label she should wear. When asked how she describes herself, Harris often says simply, "American." But part of Harris's American story includes a chapter in Canada, too. When she was twelve, she and her sister moved from sunny California to snowy Montreal when their mother was offered a cancer research position and professorship at McGill University.

The Montreal Years

In Montreal, Kamala wasted little time in picking up the activist mantle from her parents. The apartment building they lived in had strict rules. One such rule prohibited playing on the lawn. Kamala and

Maya recruited other children, and together they staged a protest against that rule. The sisters prevailed, and at age thirteen, Kamala learned a valuable lesson about fighting for what you want. The other things she learned in middle school were a little more mainstream. Her mother had enrolled her in a fine arts middle school, so Kamala dutifully learned the violin, French horn, and kettle drum, though none of those instruments interested her for very long.

Dance was another subject, however. While attending Westmount High School, she cofounded a dance troupe called Midnight Magic. The troupe performed at senior centers and at school fund-raisers and occupied many fun-filled hours a week. In her senior yearbook, Kamala refers to dancing with Midnight Magic as one of her favorite memories of high school. Kamala also excelled in her studies and carried herself in a way that made classmates and teachers think she was bound for bigger things. She "gave off an aura suggesting she was poised for success,"[12] Paul Olioff, a classmate of Kamala's and later a professor at McGill University, said in a 2018 interview with the *Toronto Star*.

What's in the Name Kamala?

Kamala, pronounced "Comma-la" (like the punctuation mark), means "lotus flower" in Sanskrit. In Indian culture the lotus is a symbol of purity, enlightenment, and rebirth. Her middle name is Devi, which in Sanskrit means "heavenly" or "divine." Harris says she is used to people mispronouncing her name when they first meet her. Justice Sonia Sotomayor even mispronounced it when she swore Harris in as vice president during the January 2021 inauguration.

But during the 2020 campaign, some opponents and critics made a point of mispronouncing *Kamala*, emphasizing the second syllable instead of the first. Harris feels very strongly about honoring people's names. She told a reporter for *People* magazine in 2020 that names are a gift a family bestows on a child and should be treated properly. "Respect the names that people are given and use those names with respect," she said. "Sometimes my team will give me an acknowledgement card, the names of people to acknowledge at events and just their title and last name is there. And I'll always say, 'What is their full name?' Maybe that comes from my own experience with my name, but I think names are very important."

Quoted in Sandra Sobieraj Westfall and Sam Gillette, "Kamala Harris Reacts to Mocking Mispronunciations of Her Name: 'It's About Respect,'" *People*, October 30, 2020. https://people.com.

Students of many racial and ethnic backgrounds roamed the halls at Westmount. There were kids from comfortable middle-class backgrounds and kids from families with little money and resources. Westmount was also a school for students who had been expelled from expensive private schools. "People had to make friends with people from places they had never even been before," Olioff said in a 2020 *Los Angeles Times* interview. "Kamala was very good at negotiating between the various communities in a very complex high school ecosystem."[13]

But Kamala did not let the cliques and drama of high school keep her from doing the right thing. In her senior year she organized a large group of girls in her class to attend prom (called "grad" at Westmount) together. She was concerned that girls who did not get asked to the dance would feel like outcasts, so she made sure the event was as fun and memorable as possible for her classmates.

Before she graduated from high school, Kamala Harris already knew she wanted to be a lawyer. Growing up listening to her Indian family talk about corruption and injustice in their country and her parents and their friends debate economics, race, women's rights, and other matters of social justice all left an impression on Harris. She had heard the story of how her mother took legal action when she was denied a teaching position at the University of California, Berkeley—likely due to racism and sexism—and always believed that fighting for victims' rights might be part of her future. "Lawyers have a profound ability and responsibility to be a voice for the vulnerable and the voiceless,"[14] she said in a 2013 interview with her law school alumni magazine.

Harris looked up to people like Constance Baker Motley, the first Black woman to argue a case before the US Supreme Court, as well as Thurgood Marshall, the first Black Supreme Court justice. Marshall, who served on the nation's highest court for twenty-four years, was a graduate of Howard University, a predominantly Black college in Washington, DC, a fact that Harris has said influenced her decision about where to attend college.

CHAPTER TWO

Harris Finds Her Voice

Harris wanted her college experience to provide not just a great education but the opportunity to become immersed in Black culture and causes. And being the daughter of parents who met during student protests in the 1960s and having grown up as an observer of political activism her whole life, it was only natural for Harris to dive into causes and pursue opportunities that reflected her values and goals. It was, in essence, her turn to use her voice.

Soon after arriving on Howard University's campus of manicured green lawns and sturdy red brick buildings in the fall of 1982, Harris participated in protests against apartheid in South Africa—just as her parents had done in Berkeley twenty years before. She later joined nearly two hundred other students in occupying a floor of the school's administration building. This action followed the university president's decision to expel the editor of the student newspaper after she published an article accusing the university of discrimination.

"Kamala had a fearlessness that, if it was something she believed in, she wanted to be actively involved, and actively engaged, and not sit on the sidelines," Gwendolyn Whitfield, a classmate of Harris's who joined her in the administration building sit-in, recalled in a 2019 *Washington Post* article. "She was unwavering in her commitment. That's what I remember. It wasn't reckless, but it was just, you know, *this* is what we should do."[15]

Harris took part in demonstrations just about every weekend during her freshman year and many more afterward at Howard. "I was born in that," Harris said of marches and protests in a 2019 *Washington Post* article. "My parents were active in the movement. So this was very familiar territory to me."[16]

Feeling Empowered

Harris felt empowered to act on her principles because she was on a campus filled with young people of color, many of whom shared her passion for social justice. Years later, in a 2019 speech to Howard students, Harris recalled the first awe-inspiring day of freshman orientation as she gazed at so many other Black students in the school's Cramton Auditorium. "I remember standing in the back of the room, looking around Cramton, and I was like, 'Oh my gosh! We're all in one place under one roof!'"[17] she said.

While at Howard, Harris also worked at several internships, including one in the office of California Democratic senator Alan Cranston. Thirty years later, Harris would run for and be elected to that same Senate seat. Howard even provided her first taste of personal campaign victory when she won a student election to be the freshman class representative on the university's Liberal Arts Student Council. On a campus filled with smart, competitive, and politically savvy students, that was considered to be quite an accomplishment. "That was my first run for public office," Harris said in a 2020 interview with *Essence* magazine. "And when you run for public office at Howard University, you can run for office anywhere."[18]

Harris, who often carried a briefcase around campus, also became president of a student club called the Abram Harris Economics Society. Through this club she worked alongside Rodney Green, a longtime economics professor with the university. "I remember she took her role very seriously,"[19] Green said in a 2020 NPR article, noting that Harris was involved in recruiting guest speakers and employers to campus and advising the economics department about its curriculum.

This role was a fitting accompaniment to Harris's interests. She had chosen a double major in political science and economics. And she had learned a great deal about economics and how it relates to social justice from her father and from her maternal grandfather, who had a long career at the highest levels of India's government.

Harris was also recruited to join the university's male-dominated debate team by the only female student on the team, Lita Rosario. Rosario had been impressed listening to Harris speak at the Punch-Out, a gathering place and small dining hall on campus where students, professors, and visitors would debate the big topics of the era. Those topics included apartheid in South Africa, civil rights in America, and President Ronald

When the time came to decide where she would go to college, Kamala chose to attend Howard University.

Reagan's administration. "She was so spirited and cogent in her arguments," Rosario told the *New York Times* in 2020. "I remember her enthusiasm. And I mostly remember that she was never intimidated."[20]

A Deep Appreciation for Howard University

Those formative years at Howard were also largely shaped by her membership in the Alpha Kappa Alpha (AKA) Sorority, the first Greek-letter organization established by and for African American college women. Harris counts her AKA sisters among her closest friends, and during her run for president and later for vice president, she made multiple appearances at joyous AKA fundraisers, festooned with streamers and balloons of pink and green, the sorority's colors. One of her early campaign stops when she was running for president in 2019 was the Pink Ice Gala, an annual AKA-sponsored community fundraiser in South Carolina. Hundreds of AKA members arrived in pink and green to support their ambitious sorority sister.

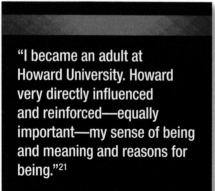

"I became an adult at Howard University. Howard very directly influenced and reinforced—equally important—my sense of being and meaning and reasons for being."[21]

—Kamala Harris

While on the campaign trail in 2020, Harris proudly shared her devotion to Howard University, too, making occasional speeches there and even working out of an office on campus. She spoke with great admiration and appreciation for what Howard provided her. "I became an adult at Howard University," Harris said in a 2019 *Washington Post* interview. "Howard very directly influenced and reinforced—equally important—my sense of being and meaning and reasons for being."[21]

Harris is passionate about the need for individuals to stand up for their beliefs. Consistent with this view, in February 2019 she urged a group of Howard students to use their voices to speak out and their feet to march when necessary. The candi-

Kamala Harris graduated from Howard University in 1986. Howard is the oldest and among the largest historically Black colleges and universities in the nation. There are about one hundred public and private HBCUs, as these academic institutions are often known. They were originally established to provide a college education for Black students, many of whom would have been denied that opportunity before the passage of the 1964 Civil Rights Act. Long after the first HBCUs were established, they have remained a vibrant component of US academic institutions of higher learning. Research suggests that Black students at HBCUs tend to have higher graduation rates than their peers at other schools and that HBCUs foster a safer learning environment where Black students often feel more comfortable expressing themselves. "What you learn at an HBCU is you do not have to fit into someone's limited perspective of what it means to be young, gifted and Black," Harris said in a 2018 interview.

Quoted in Fredreka Schouten, "'She's Our DNA': How Kamala Harris' Presidential Bid Is Inspiring a Network of Immigrants to Donate, Volunteer," CNN, March 31, 2019. www.cnn.com.

date reminded her audience about her experience with sit-ins and apartheid demonstrations, and how issues of race and discrimination will always need vocal, dedicated champions. She said:

> These are the moments in time that are going to require us to step up and stand out and speak up. Years from now, you're going to look back on these days. . . . I want that you will be able to talk about not just how you felt but what action you took—what you did, how you spoke up, how you stood out, how you marched when necessary, how you shouted when necessary. How you made your university proud, and how you continued in the tradition of the great Howard University.[22]

On to Law School

After graduation from Howard in 1986, Harris returned to California and enrolled at the University of California, Hastings College of the

Law, in San Francisco. While in law school, she lived with her sister, Maya, and Maya's baby daughter. Maya was working toward a degree from the University of California, Berkeley at the same time.

Harris wasn't entirely sure what type of law she wanted to practice during her first year at Hastings. She had known for some time, however, that lawyers were looked to as problem solvers. Growing up she personally knew two lawyers; one was an uncle and the other a family friend. Whenever a friend or family member had a problem, someone would suggest calling one of them because they would know how to handle the situation. "I wanted to be able to do that," she wrote in her memoir. "I wanted to be the one people called. I wanted to be the one who could help."[23]

While at Hastings, Harris continued in the activist role she had assumed at Howard, serving as president of the school's Black Law Students Association (BLSA) and holding a regional post with the group's national parent organization. The BLSA was formed to help meet the educational, social, and professional needs of Black

In 2019, during a campaign appearance in Birmingham, Alabama, Harris posed for a photo with fellow members of Alpha Kappa Alpha Sorority, the first Greek-letter organization founded by and for African American college women.

When it came time to pick a sorority at Howard University, there was little doubt that Kamala Harris would pledge Alpha Kappa Alpha. "My Aunt Chris, who was the one who really had a big influence on me, was an AKA and pledged at Howard," Harris said in a 2020 interview with *Essence*. "So it was just very natural for me to want to end up pledging in the sorority which I feel really rounded out my experience. It's a sisterhood that lasts till today." When Harris announced that she was running for president in 2019, her line sisters—the women who pledged AKA during the same year at Howard—jumped in to help. They hosted fund-raisers and did whatever they could for the woman they long ago nicknamed C3 for "cool, calm, and collected." "We are sort of a fine-tuned machine," line sister Karyn Upshaw said in a 2020 interview. Upshaw was one of several line sisters to attend Harris's victory speech in Wilmington, Delaware, after the November 2020 election. "We really take our pledge to heart and we help each other. Even for her presidency, and then for the Biden-Harris ticket, we buckled down. We did a lot of voter registration support and things to help her and help our country get to the place where we are today."

Quoted in Tanya A. Christian, "HBCU Love: Kamala Harris Says Attending Howard Was a Childhood Dream," *Essence*, May 15, 2020. www.essence.com.

Quoted in Shawn Yancy and Briana Trujillo, "From Howard to VP: Kamala Harris Alpha Kappa Alpha Sisters Keep Her Centered," NBC4 Washington, January 18, 2021. www.nbcwashington.com.

law students and advocate for the legal community to better address the needs of the Black community. She also served as an advocate for greater campus diversity as part of the school's Legal Education Opportunity Program, which works to make law school more accessible to minorities, low-income students, and others.

Jeff Adachi, a former San Francisco public defender, met Harris in law school and was immediately impressed by her. In a May 2019 article in the *Atlantic*, Adachi recalled the law student he would later clash with on and off for years in San Francisco courtrooms. "Did she always have the charm and ambition she's known for today? Yeah,"[24] he said.

Setting Her Sights on Being a Prosecutor

Though Harris knew she wanted to pursue a career in law and public service, it was not until she spent a summer interning at the Alameda County District Attorney's Office that her focus sharpened on becoming a prosecutor. In a criminal court, a prosecutor brings charges against people suspected of crimes and makes the case for their conviction. Harris's decision to become a prosecutor was not readily embraced by her family and friends. At a time when people of color were being disproportionately arrested and charged with crimes and mass incarceration was devastating Black communities, many Black and immigrant people viewed the police and prosecutors as major contributors to the problem.

While Harris was well aware of that dynamic, she saw herself as someone who could help change things from the inside rather than as an advocate for change from the outside. "When activists came marching and banging on doors," Harris wrote in her memoirs, "I wanted to be on the other side to let them in. . . . For too long, we'd been told that there were only two options: to be either tough on crime or soft on crime."[25] Harris describes such thinking as a false choice, arguing that, for example, assault and other violent crimes should be treated much more seriously and aggressively than "victimless" crimes such as minor drug possession.

She even had to defend her decision to her mother, arguing that her focus would be on bringing to justice those who would hurt or exploit innocent people. Harris was not surprised that her friends and family did not initially support her desire to become a prosecutor. She grew up hearing stories about charges being brought against people of color without much evidence and of prosecutors withholding evidence that could help defendants. But in her memoirs, Harris explained the other side of being a prosecutor. She noted the courageous prosecutors who went after the Ku Klux Klan in the South and who sought to put an end to the actions of corrupt politicians and polluters. She wrote, "I knew that equal justice was an aspiration. I knew that the force of the law was applied unevenly, sometimes by design. But I also knew that what was wrong with the system didn't need to be an immutable fact. And I wanted to be part of changing that."[26]

CHAPTER THREE

A Rising Star

Harris's first job out of law school in 1990 was as a deputy district attorney in Alameda County, California. Alameda County, home to both Oakland and Berkeley, is one of the most ethnically diverse regions in the San Francisco Bay Area. And it was familiar territory for Harris, who had spent part of her childhood there and then studied law in nearby San Francisco.

In her new job, Harris specialized in prosecuting child sexual assault cases, a subject that had become important to her while still in high school. One of Harris's closest high school friends, Wanda Kagan, tearfully told Harris one day that she had been molested by her own father. After Harris told her mother the shocking news, Shyamala Gopalan urged Kagan to live with them until she graduated from high school. "One of the reasons I wanted to be a prosecutor was to protect people like her,"[27] Harris posted on Instagram in the fall of 2020. Kagan remains close to the Harris family, still moved by the love and support they provided during those difficult times. "They planted a seed of stability and empowerment in me,"[28] says Kagan, now a hospital administrator in Montreal.

Having honed her skills as a prosecutor, Harris moved across the bay in 1998 to become an assistant district attorney in San Francisco. She prosecuted cases involving homicide, robbery, burglary, and sexual assault. In her role as an advocate for crime victims, Harris frequently put in long days before going to court so that she could put forward the strongest case possible. Suzy Loftus, an attorney who worked with Harris in San Francisco, says the future vice president was extremely tough but fair in the courtroom. "She's intense to be questioned by," Loftus says. "A prosecutor's training is to be prepared and know the answer to every question before it's asked."[29] Having proved to be an exceptionally tough and skilled prosecutor, Harris was named managing attorney of the Career Criminal Unit of the San Francisco District Attorney's Office. She prosecuted serial felony offenders, individuals who had been arrested for serious crimes multiple times.

"She's intense to be questioned by. A prosecutor's training is to be prepared and know the answer to every question before it's asked."[29]

—Suzy Loftus, a former colleague of Kamala Harris

When it came to young offenders, Harris believed they should be treated differently from adults. She focused on helping them turn their lives around and giving them a chance at a better future. In combating teenage prostitution, Harris put more of an emphasis on treating young girls as victims rather than criminals and pushed for tougher penalties on the men who took advantage of the teens. She took a controversial stand on a statewide ballot measure called Proposition 21. It called for tougher penalties for crimes committed by people under age eighteen. One of the changes would allow youths charged with serious crimes to be tried as adults. Many law enforcement officers and district attorney offices around the state supported the measure, but Harris believed it was wrong. She volunteered in the campaign against its passage. But in 2000 California voters approved the measure. Disappointed, but undeterred, Harris remained committed to fighting on behalf of children and families.

A Run for San Francisco District Attorney

During that time, some friction arose in the San Francisco District Attorney's Office. Some people were jealous of Harris, who was becoming well known in the city and was often the person reporters covering the courts sought to interview. Though she denied it at the time, there were also suspicions that she was planning to run for the office of San Francisco district attorney in the 2003 election. If she ran for this office, her opponent would be Terrence Hallinan, the man who had recruited her from Alameda County.

Hallinan planned to reassign Harris to a different role in the district attorney's office, a change that would have been seen as a demotion. Instead, in August 2000 Harris resigned and left for a job as head of the San Francisco City Attorney's Child and Family Services Division. That position allowed her to continue her efforts on behalf of children who had fallen victim to abuse, brutality, neglect, and other similar crimes. "These are just wonderful children who at no fault of their own have been abused or neglected, and really need that kind of commitment and that sense of responsibility from the community,"[30] Harris said in a 2002 interview.

Frustrated with the way the San Francisco District Attorney's Office was being run and hoping to reassert herself as one of the top prosecutors in the state, Harris decided to run against Hallinan.

As a prosecutor, Harris worked to combat teenage prostitution by treating young girls as victims, rather than criminals.

A third candidate, well-known San Francisco attorney Bill Fazio, also entered the race. During her campaign, Harris said she would be more competent and effective than Hallinan while still sharing many of his priorities, including making victims' rights a priority. It was a long-shot bid for the high-profile office, but Harris had two secret weapons: her conviction that she could do the job better and her mother. Gopalan joined her daughter's campaign immediately and drove Harris to campaign events, managed volunteers, and spoke at rallies, urging voters to have the same faith in her daughter as she did.

Though her star had been rising for a few years, Harris had the lowest name recognition of the three candidates. So she left nothing to chance. Her plan was to simply outwork her opponents. "I'd walk up and down the hills and knock on doors," she said in a 2019 *Politico* article. "I'd stand at bus stops starting at 6 in the morning until 8 at night, begging people to talk to me on their way to work."[31] And it was not unusual to see Harris driving around the city with a stack of posters, a roll of duct tape,

Environmental Champion

Kamala Harris made environmental protection a priority throughout her time as San Francisco's district attorney and as California's attorney general. In 2004 she charged two men with dumping hundreds of gallons of printer's ink into a creek that ran through San Francisco's Bayview neighborhood. A year later she established an environmental crimes unit, which helped the city recover millions of dollars from polluters large and small. As attorney general, she secured a $44 million settlement to cover damages caused when an oil tanker collided with the San Francisco–Oakland Bay Bridge, spilling 50,000 gallons (189,271 L) of fuel into the bay. Also as attorney general, Harris went after major petroleum companies such as Chevron, BP, and ARCO to resolve allegations that they failed to manage hazardous waste in underground storage units around the state. In the run-up to the 2020 presidential election, Tiernan Sittenfeld, vice president of the environmental organization League of Conservation Voters, said, "Senator Harris has been a longtime champion for climate action and environmental justice. . . . We know she will continue the fight for a more just solution to the climate crisis."

Quoted in Marianne Lavelle, "On Climate, Kamala Harris Has a Record and Profile for Action," Inside Climate News, August 12, 2020. https://insideclimatenews.org.

campaign brochures, and her ironing board in the backseat. She would pull up to a store or library, set up her ironing board, tape a couple of posters to it, set out some flyers, and talk to whomever would stop by. "Ironing boards were the first standing desks,"[32] she said in *Politico*.

Harris won by a large margin. She became the city's first Black district attorney and the first woman to hold that position. She successfully ran for reelection in 2007.

Changing the Nature of the Office

As district attorney, Harris continued to be tough on violent crime and advocate for victims. But she also sought ways to reduce recidivism, the return to crime by people who have already been through the criminal justice system. In 2005 she launched a program called Back on Track, which allowed certain offenders (those without a history of gang involvement or gun violence) to plead guilty but instead of getting jail time be sent to a six-week "boot camp" in order to complete 220 hours of community service and develop a plan to turn their lives around. They could get a GED (a high school diploma equivalent), career training and job placement, money management lessons, anger management therapy, and help with parenting and child support.

The program proved to be successful at helping offenders chart a new path as well as saving the city money by not having to jail these individuals. In a 2007 interview, Harris said, "We charge them for committing a crime. They go to a courtroom and plead guilty because they did commit a crime. This is about accountability. There's no fiction here. You did commit a crime. Accept it. Own up to it. Then let's talk about what we can do to change circumstances going forward."[33]

Programs such as Back on Track attracted positive interest and attention around the state. Harris was becoming known as a progressive, innovative prosecutor. But like anyone in a high-profile job, she had her share of critics and crises. At one point

In 2004 Harris became San Francisco's first Black district attorney as well as the first woman elected to that position.

someone working in an evidence lab in the district attorney's office stole drugs that had been evidence in ongoing cases. Public defenders and criminal defense attorneys criticized Harris for not being forthcoming about these problems in her office. Eventually, many cases had to be thrown out due to a lack of evidence.

Harris also drew complaints about a 2006 truancy program targeting the families of students who frequently skipped school. Statistics showed a link between habitual school truancy and crime. As part of the program, parents of truant children could be criminally charged. Seven parents were ultimately charged, though no one ever went to jail. Harris defended the program, noting that it gave families resources to improve high school graduation rates. By the spring of 2009, the number of habitually truant elementary school students in the city was less than half of what it had been in 2006.

One of the biggest controversies during her years as San Francisco district attorney occurred just three months after she started the job. A young police officer was killed in the line of duty. Harris had long been an opponent of the death penalty. It was her belief that life in prison was a more severe punishment than death. When she announced that she would not seek the death penalty in the officer's killing, that decision was roundly criticized. At a service for the slain officer, California senator Dianne Feinstein declared that the person convicted of murdering the officer should receive the death penalty. Hundreds of police officers in attendance greeted that statement with a standing ovation. The San Francisco Police Union never endorsed Harris again in any of her local or statewide races.

California Attorney General

Harris managed to rise above those controversies and position herself as a strong candidate for California attorney general. She had the backing of the state's two Democratic senators, House Speaker Nancy Pelosi (from San Francisco), and other prominent Californians. In 2010 Harris narrowly won the position, making her the state's first woman, Black, and South Asian American to be California attorney general. And as she had in San Francisco, Harris won reelection four years later.

As the state's top law enforcement officer, Harris earned praise for a number of high-profile achievements, including helping victims of the financial crisis that began in 2008. Some of the country's largest financial institutions had been accused of taking advantage of homebuyers, many of whom were soon unable to make their mortgage payments. Millions of homes across the country then went into foreclosure, a situation in which the banks that made the home loans took control of the properties. Under pressure from homeowners to accept a $4 billion settlement from the country's largest mortgage companies, Harris refused and pressed harder. Eventually, the settlement came in at $20 billion. "It's not just about how much money was in the settlement," says Senator Elizabeth

Who Is Maya Harris?

From the moment she was born, Maya Harris has had a devoted big sister looking out for her, playing with her, and later relying on her wisdom and energy. Kamala Harris listens closely to the advice of her little sister, who may not have the name recognition of her famous sibling but has nevertheless forged an impressive career on her own. After graduating from the University of California, Berkeley in 1989, Maya went straight to Stanford Law School and was later named editor of the *Stanford Law Review*. She went on to work in civil and criminal litigation with a San Francisco law firm while also serving as an adjunct law professor with the University of San Francisco School of Law. And at age twenty-nine, she was named dean of the Lincoln Law School of San Jose, making her one of the youngest law school deans in US history. She followed that with high-profile work with the American Civil Liberties Union and the Ford Foundation. Maya Harris went on to be a senior policy adviser on Hillary Clinton's 2016 presidential campaign and chair of her sister's presidential campaign. She continues to be a leading public policy advocate and a trusted—and beloved—adviser to the vice president.

Warren. "It's how aggressively Kamala and her team stayed after the banks to make sure they followed through."[34] Similarly, Harris succeeded in getting settlements from for-profit colleges accused of scamming students, promising them a quality of education and career opportunities that the schools did not deliver.

Harris also sought to make law enforcement more transparent to the public. She created Open Justice, an online platform that provides details about law enforcement practices and statistics around the state. She hoped it would make police departments more accountable by releasing data on the numbers of deaths and injuries suffered by people in police custody. Still, many critics contend Harris did not do enough to reform California's criminal justice system, reduce the state's prison population, and address misconduct by law enforcement officers and prosecutors. Harris has defended her record, pointing out that she was successful in many of her reform efforts,

"It's not just about how much money was in the settlement. It's how aggressively Kamala and her team stayed after the banks to make sure they followed through."[34]

—Elizabeth Warren, US senator

such as instituting a racial bias training program for police officers and supporting programs that channeled some offenders into work training programs instead of prison. But she has also noted that as attorney general, she was bound to enforce the laws of the state, even if she did not always agree with them.

Marriage and Companionship

Harris's work as attorney general occupied a great deal of her time, leaving little time or energy for life outside of work. But her friends were looking out for her. In 2013, on a blind date set up by a mutual friend, Harris met a successful entertainment attorney from Southern California named Douglas Emhoff. The two soon

Less than a year after meeting in 2013, Harris and Douglas Emhoff were married.

became inseparable. The morning after their first date, Emhoff emailed her, saying, "I really like you, and I want to see if we can make this work."[35]

They were married less than a year later in a small service officiated by Harris's sister, Maya. Of Emhoff, Harris told the online news show *Now This* in July 2019, "He is funny. He is kind. He is patient. He loves my cooking. He's just a really great guy."[36]

Harris became stepmother to Emhoff's two children from his first marriage. They were both teenagers when their father and Harris married, and they affectionately refer to her as "Momala."

Emhoff later proved to be an important source of encouragement and support, as well as an effective campaigner. Their first effort campaigning together came along quickly—the 2016 race for the US Senate seat left open by the retirement of Senator Barbara Boxer. This was the same Senate seat once held by Harris's one-time boss, Alan Cranston. At the time, Harris said that she wanted to take the fight she had led in defense of California's families and environment to the national level. She sought greater say in economic matters, which fall to lawmakers who approve budgets and tax policy. "I will be a fighter for middle-class families who are feeling the pinch of stagnant wages and diminishing opportunity," Harris said in a message launching her Senate campaign. "I will be a fighter for our children who deserve a world-class education, and for students burdened by predatory lenders and skyrocketing tuition. And I will fight relentlessly to protect our coast, our immigrant communities and our seniors."[37]

> "I will be a fighter for middle-class families who are feeling the pinch of stagnant wages and diminishing opportunity."[37]
>
> —Kamala Harris

CHAPTER FOUR

Senator Harris

When Harris entered the Senate race in January 2015, California had a new election system in which the top two vote getters during the primaries would be on the ballot in the November 2016 general election, regardless of their political party. It turned out that Harris and another Democrat, Loretta Sanchez, received the most votes in the primaries, marking the first time that no Republican would be on the ballot for Senate since Californians began directly electing their senators in 1914.

Along the way, Harris received endorsements from President Barack Obama and Vice President Joe Biden. She had become good friends with Biden's son Beau, who was the attorney general of Delaware and been an early ally in Harris's efforts to hold the big banks more accountable for their role in the recent economic crisis. She ran on issues such as reforming the criminal justice system, protecting the rights of LGBTQ individuals, improving access to higher education, ensuring equal pay for equal work, and protecting the coastlines and other environmentally sensitive areas of California and the country.

Harris Wins a US Senate Seat

Harris won by a large margin, making her just the second African American woman elected to the Senate and the first South Asian American in Senate history. But election night proved to be bittersweet. Harris was elected to the Senate on November 8, 2016—the same night Republican Donald Trump was elected president. Harris had spoken out repeatedly against many of Trump's ideas and statements, particularly his thoughts on immigration—a subject close to Harris's heart. As the daughter of immigrants, Harris believed that people seeking a better life in the United States should be given that opportunity. Harris had also seen firsthand in her home state that immigrants are very important to the economy but are often mistreated by employers and law enforcement.

On election night 2016, realizing that Trump was likely to defeat Hillary Clinton—whom Harris had advised throughout the campaign—Harris abandoned much of her own victory speech at a rally in Los Angeles and vowed to stand up against Trump's agenda. At one point she said, "When our ideals and fundamental values are being attacked, do we retreat or do we fight? I say we fight."[38]

And fight she did. Just one day after Trump's January 2017 inauguration, Harris was a key speaker at the Women's March on Washington, DC, reminding the massive crowd that true power lies in the hands of the people, not the politicians. "It's going to be harder before it gets easier," she said. "I know we will rise to the challenge and I know we will keep fighting no matter what. This was a day for all of us to come together in our nation's capital. . . . Let's buckle in because it's going to be a bumpy ride."[39]

> "When our ideals and fundamental values are being attacked, do we retreat or do we fight? I say we fight."[38]
>
> —Kamala Harris

Battles on Capitol Hill

The opposition to Trump and his decisions and policies never seemed to let up. A month into his term, Trump announced a temporary ban on refugees and other people from seven predominantly Muslim countries entering the United States. It was a chaotic time, with people arriving in airports being detained. Law-

In 2016 Harris campaigned to become one of California's two US senators.

yers from around the country descended on the airports trying to volunteer their services to help those in detention. To try to bring some order, Harris filed her first bill in the Senate. It was meant to guarantee legal access for the people detained after arriving in the United States. Harris had seen migrant children caught up in the legal system after crossing the border into California, only to have little or no representation in immigration courts. "This is about due process, a fundamental principle on which our system of justice is based," she told her fellow senators. "It's about saying, 'Let's make these individuals have a fair opportunity to go through the process in a way that the outcome will be just.'"[40]

Harris also strongly advocated for the young people in the Deferred Action for Childhood Arrivals (DACA) program, which provided protection against deportation for individuals who were brought into the United States without documentation as kids. Most of them were the children of parents who were undocumented immigrants and had spent much of their lives in fear of

Visit to a Refugee Camp

A few months after taking office in 2017, Kamala Harris took her first trip overseas as a US senator. Already well traveled from her visits to family around the world as a young girl, Harris made a much different journey this time. She flew to the Middle East to visit with troops from her home state of California stationed in Iraq and then to a Syrian refugee camp in Jordan. The camp was filled with people who had fled the horrors of the Syrian civil war. Many had hoped to find refuge in America but were stranded when Trump imposed the travel ban. A Syrian father told Harris of the horrors in his home country and how he lost his daughter to the violence there. "When I think about that in the context of a policy we have in our country that says we're going to shut our border to these refugees mostly because of their religion, I am as offended and disturbed as I was before, if not more so," she told a reporter upon returning home.

Quoted in ABC7, "Sen. Kamala Harris Visits Troops, Refugee Camp in Middle East," April 17, 2017. https://abc7.com.

being arrested and deported. Harris pushed for greater protection for DACA recipients (known as Dreamers), especially after Trump tried to rescind the program in the fall of 2017. "They come to my office every day panicked," Harris told a reporter with *Vogue* about individuals in the DACA program, many of whom had become teachers, soldiers, college students, nurses, and doctors. "These DACA kids don't know what tomorrow will bring, except that it will require them to leave the only place they've ever known to go somewhere they have no recollection of ever being."[41]

Harris repeatedly pushed for a DACA bill that would give the young people a clear path to citizenship. It became a key campaign issue for her later on. Eric Garcetti, the mayor of Los Angeles—the city with the most Dreamers in the United States—called Harris "the strongest ally we have in the fight."[42]

Not every moment in the Senate was a battle for Harris. She took great pride in mentoring the young people on her staff and those who worked in various capacities on Capitol Hill. During a 2018 meeting with recent college graduates who had earned fellowships with the Congressional Hispanic Caucus Institute, she talked about her days as a Senate intern—and ultimately being elected to that same Senate seat. "So you *neva know*,"[43] she told them and urged them to look around at what could be their futures.

But the battles on Capitol Hill continued as the DACA debate moved to the courts, the travel ban remained in place, and other matters continued to confront Congress. Harris often found herself stepping back into her role as a prosecutor as the Senate tried to be a check on the executive branch.

Showing No Fear

In her four years as a US senator, Harris relied on her finely honed courtroom skills, developing a reputation as a tough questioner during committee hearings. She emerged as someone who would not be overwhelmed by the job or intimidated by others in power.

In 2017, as a member of the Senate Intelligence Committee, Harris grilled then–attorney general Jeff Sessions about contacts he may have had with Russian officials while he campaigned for Trump in 2016 as a senator from Alabama. The committee was investigating reports that there may have been improper contact between the Trump campaign and Russia. When Sessions declined to give her straight answers, Harris kept peppering him with rapid-fire questions. Flustered, Sessions responded, "I don't want to be rushed this fast. It makes me nervous."[44]

Republicans on the committee interrupted Harris and chastised her for not letting Sessions answer, just as they had done days before when she took a similar approach to Rod Rosenstein, the deputy attorney general, regarding his role in Trump's firing of the director of the Federal Bureau of Investigation, James Comey. The incidents sparked considerable media coverage. Democrats applauded Harris's aggressive style, while Republicans accused her of trying to score political points rather than get answers. Many observers took note that Harris, one of the few women on the committee, was the only person admonished by her Republican colleagues.

Undaunted, two years later Harris famously challenged another attorney general, William Barr. This exchange took place after

As a member of the Senate's Intelligence Committee, Harris grilled Attorney General Jeff Sessions (shown with Donald Trump in 2016) regarding contacts he might have had with Russian officials during Trump's run for the presidency.

the release of an independent counsel investigation into possible illegal contact between the Trump campaign and Russia in 2016 and a potential cover-up following the campaign. The independent counsel's report cited actions by the president that could be construed as obstruction of justice but made no recommendation on whether or not to file such a charge. Barr opted against charging Trump with obstruction.

During a hearing before the Senate Judiciary Committee, Barr would not answer Harris's questions about whether he or someone in his office had actually reviewed the evidence in the report before making that decision. After fumbling in trying to explain his reasoning, which did not sound convincing to the senator from California, the steely-eyed Harris sternly said, "I think you've made it clear, sir, that you have not looked at the evidence and we can move on."[45]

Taking a Stand

Harris took other strong stands in the Senate. She joined several other Democratic senators in calling for the removal of White House adviser Stephen Miller after it was learned that he had promoted White nationalist content on a right-wing website. Harris was also an outspoken critic of the Republican leadership in the Senate for their unwillingness to compromise on COVID-19 relief legislation and for their push to have conservative judges, many of them deemed unqualified, approved for lifelong federal judicial posts.

Because Republicans held the majority of Senate seats, Harris and the Democrats were often on the losing side of these debates. But Harris, who had urged her allies to prepare for a rough road ahead, continued leading the way on issues close to her heart. Her dedication to immigration reform and more humane policies toward migrants took center stage in 2018, when the

Seeking Justice for Lynching Victims

As part of her long-standing commitment to justice for crime victims, Harris co-sponsored a bill that would make lynching a federal hate crime. The Justice for Victims of Lynching Act of 2018 would have given judges leeway to impose harsher sentences for people convicted of carrying out a lynching. The bill also called for the United States to acknowledge the failures of past administrations to prevent lynchings. "We finally have a chance to speak the truth about our past, and make clear that these hateful acts should never happen again without serious, severe, and swift consequences and accountability," Harris said in a December 2018 speech to the Senate.

Though the bill passed unanimously in the Senate, the House of Representatives rejected a companion bill. Senator Rand Paul of Kentucky later tried to alter the language of a revised bill that had been submitted for consideration. An emotional Harris responded, "Senator Paul is now trying to weaken a bill that was already passed. There's no reason for this." The bill was not revived before Harris left the Senate, but she and President Biden have vowed to devote more resources to preventing and prosecuting hate crimes in any form.

Quoted in PR Lockhart, "After More than 200 Attempts, the Senate Has Finally Passed Anti-Lynching Legislation," Vox, December 21, 2018. www.vox.com.

Quoted in Clare Foran and Lauren Fox, "Emotional Debate Erupts Over Anti-Lynching Legislation as Cory Booker and Kamala Harris Speak Out Against Rand Paul Amendement," CNN, June 4, 2020. www.cnn.com.

Trump administration took a hard line against migrants crossing the border. A policy in which children were separated from their families created a storm of controversy, and Harris became one of the Senate's most outspoken critics of family separation.

During an April 2018 hearing with then-secretary of the US Department of Homeland Security (DHS) Kirstjen Nielsen, Harris cited an American Academy of Pediatrics report that stated children separated from their families could suffer long-term emotional harm. She repeatedly challenged Nielsen's assertions that the policy did not lead to the detention of children when an inspector general's report stated the opposite. As more evidence emerged

Harris addresses a crowd protesting against the Trump administration's policy of separating migrant children from their families.

that the DHS and specifically the US Customs and Border Protection were engaged in morally questionable activities, Harris became the first senator to call for Nielsen's resignation. "The government should be in the business of keeping families together, not tear-

ing them apart," Harris said in a statement in June 2018. "And the government should have a commitment to transparency and accountability. Under Secretary Nielsen's tenure, the Department of Homeland Security has a track record of neither. As a result, she must resign."[46]

Other Democrats joined Harris, and eventually the DHS changed its family-separation policy and Nielsen resigned, though not until the following year. But by now it was clear that Harris was emerging as one of the toughest leaders in her party. Even Republican Senate colleagues admired Harris's determination and drive. Before she became Biden's choice as running mate, Harris received praise from Republican senator Lindsey Graham, a frequent sparring partner on the Senate Judiciary Committee and on the Senate floor. "She's hard-nosed. She's smart. She's tough,"[47] Graham said.

Just two years into her first term in the Senate, and having established herself as a rising star in the Democratic Party, Harris decided she was ready for a much bigger stage. In early 2019 she joined a list of Democratic Party luminaries in seeking to be the nominee to unseat Donald Trump in his bid for a second term in office.

CHAPTER FIVE

The Remarkable Path to the White House

Having earned a reputation as a smart, tough senator who seemed to be unafraid to challenge President Trump and members of his administration, Harris joined dozens of other Democratic hopefuls who sought their party's nomination for president beginning in 2019. "I love my country, and this is a moment in time that I feel a sense of responsibility to fight for the best of who we are,"[48] Harris said in announcing her candidacy on ABC's *Good Morning America*.

She made her announcement on Martin Luther King Jr. Day, which was done intentionally. Her campaign explained that the timing was meant to remind voters of the fight for progress that characterized Harris's early years and her work as a prosecutor and senator. A week later, in a return to her hometown of Oakland, Harris appeared before an overflow crowd of more than twenty thousand people gathered at city hall—about a mile from the hospital where she was born. "My whole life, I've only had one client: the people,"[49] Harris said, reminding the crowd of her career as a prosecutor and a victims' advocate. From the beginning of her presidential campaign, Harris used a phrase she spoke to judges in the courtroom during her district attorney days, introducing herself as a representative of the public. When the judge would call on her, she would say, "Kamala Harris, for the people."[50] The phrase appeared on campaign posters, T-shirts, and other merchandise.

But because of her career as a prosecutor and attorney general, some Democrats were hesitant to support her. Videos of police officers using excessive force, particularly on people of color, were getting national attention, and calls for massive changes to law enforcement agencies and the criminal justice system were getting louder in 2019. "Kamala is a cop"[51] became a widely used phrase by people distrustful of how her career as a district attorney who put a lot of people behind bars fit with her campaign messages calling for major criminal justice reform.

Harris acknowledged the concerns that she might not be the candidate to help usher in such changes, but she suggested that law and order are important for any society. "I think it is a false choice to suggest that communities do not want law enforcement," Harris said in an ABC News interview. "Most communities do. They don't want excessive force. They don't want racial profiling, but then nobody should."[52]

> "I think it is a false choice to suggest that communities do not want law enforcement. Most communities do. They don't want excessive force. They don't want racial profiling, but then nobody should."[52]
>
> —Kamala Harris

Aiming for the Political Middle Ground

Harris sought to stake out the middle ground politically between the more progressive and more conservative sides of the Democratic Party. But that proved to be a difficult balancing act, since she was never able to attract enough support from throughout the party to mount a serious challenge to Joe Biden and Bernie Sanders—both of whom were considered to be the frontrunners. She did, however, make an early impression on voters and on Biden when all the Democratic candidates assembled for their first debate in June 2019.

At one point during the debate, Biden noted his ability to work with people who have very different perspectives from his own. He noted that early in his Senate career he had even managed to have civil working relationships with noted segregationist senators James Eastland of Mississippi and Herman Talmadge of Georgia. Harris jumped on this comment, describing how she had been bused across town as a kindergarten student and why that and other efforts at integration were so important. "There was a little girl in California who was part of the second class to integrate her public schools, and she was bused to school every day. And that little girl was me,"[53] Harris said, challenging Biden, who had been an opponent of federally mandated busing programs to achieve racial integration in the 1970s.

At the time, it looked like Harris and Biden would be real adversaries on the campaign trail, but no real fireworks followed. A short time later Biden said he admired Harris's intelligence and passion for social justice. After a well-received announcement and a good performance in the first debate, Harris was never quite able to break through the pack and become a viable competitor to Biden and Sanders. Lagging in the polls and unable to raise enough money to finance a national campaign, Harris used the 2019 Thanksgiving holiday weekend to consult with her campaign staff and family. Rather than push on into the early primaries that were set to begin in February 2020, Harris decided to bow out. She declared that while she was out of the race, she was not out of the fight. Her fellow candidates congratulated her on a tough campaign and for being a formidable competitor. Even Biden, perhaps foreshadowing his interest in teaming up with Harris down the road, told reporters covering the Iowa caucus, "She is a first-rate intellect, a first-rate candidate and a real competitor. I have mixed emotions

> "There was a little girl in California who was part of the second class to integrate her public schools, and she was bused to school every day. And that little girl was me."[53]
>
> —Kamala Harris

During one of the Democratic presidential debates, Harris clashed with Joe Biden (far left) over his opposition in the 1970s to busing as a means of achieving racial integration in schools.

about it because she is a really solid, solid person and loaded with talent. I'm sure she's not dropping out on wanting to make the changes she cares about."[54]

The Biden-Harris 2020 Ticket

As 2019 gave way to 2020, the political landscape was about to change dramatically. Trump was facing an impeachment trial in the Senate, having been formally impeached by the House of Representatives in December. And the COVID-19 pandemic was only a few months away from changing the way candidates campaigned, not to mention the way people around the world lived their lives. The pandemic meant the candidates would have to forgo big rallies—though Trump held many big rallies, even as many public health officials criticized the events as dangerous. In-person events were also curtailed as simple acts like shaking hands were discouraged to help slow the spread of the coronavirus that caused COVID-19.

The Job of the Vice President

The vice president has two primary duties. The first is to be ready to take over in case the president dies, resigns, or is unable to fulfill his or her duties in office. The second is presiding over the Senate. This usually means breaking a 50-50 tie. Although this does not happen often, it is more likely to happen while Harris is in office because the Senate currently has fifty Republicans and fifty Democrats. Despite this role, the vice president cannot address the Senate unless he or she is formally invited to do so.

The vice president also has many unofficial duties, most of which are determined in conversations with the president. One is to represent the president in meetings with foreign leaders or at other big events. A vice president with certain expertise or experience may be put in charge of various White House programs. Former vice president Al Gore, for example, was known as an expert on government policy and was therefore tasked by President Bill Clinton to spearhead an effort to make the federal government more efficient. And when Joe Biden, a long-time senator, was Barack Obama's vice president, Obama relied on him to work with members of Congress on bills or other priorities of the White House.

As the final few primaries wound down in the spring of 2020, it became apparent that Biden would have enough delegates to secure his party's nomination. Most of the other candidates who had dropped out of the race—including Harris—endorsed Biden as the person who could defeat Trump and begin to unify a fractured country. Then the question turned to whom Biden would choose as a running mate.

Biden had already announced that he would choose a woman as a running mate, and Harris was viewed as a top contender. But her clash with Biden during the debates and concerns about how well she could motivate more voters to turn out to the polls caused some Democrats to push for other choices.

After vetting several possible running mates, Biden and his campaign staff decided that Harris was the right choice. So on August 11, 2020, Biden made the historic announcement. He referred to her as a "fearless fighter for the little guy, and one of the country's finest public servants."[55] Later Harris tweeted that Biden would "unify the American people" and "build an America that lives up to our ideals."[56]

Harris's selection as running mate even got an immediate thumbs-up from former president Barack Obama, who tweeted, "She's spent her career defending our Constitution and fighting for folks who need a fair shake. This a good day for our country."[57]

Later that summer, due to COVID-19 concerns, the Democrats held a mostly virtual national convention to officially choose their nominees for president and vice president. In her acceptance speech, Harris showed her readiness to take on Trump. "At every step of the way, I've been guided by the words I spoke from the first time I stood in a courtroom: Kamala Harris, For the People," she said. "I've fought for children, and survivors of sexual assault. I've fought against transnational gangs. I took on the biggest banks, and helped take down one of the biggest for-profit colleges. I know a predator when I see one."[58]

In choosing Harris for his running mate, Joe Biden cited her devotion to public service and her efforts on behalf of the "little guy."

The Election

Though the Biden-Harris ticket led the polls throughout the campaign, Democratic political observers were wary. Four years earlier, polls had shown Democrat Hillary Clinton with a solid lead over Trump. Although Clinton had won the popular vote, Trump had won in the Electoral College and thus won the presidency. Furthermore, he had a solid base of support and had been able to tout a healthy economy before the COVID-19 pandemic led to major unemployment and business closings around the nation. Painting Trump as a divisive and dangerous figure, Biden and Harris presented themselves as the ticket that could unite the nation and heal social and economic wounds.

As a woman of color and daughter of immigrants, Harris and her story appealed to a broad swath of the electorate. At a Democratic fund-raiser in September 2020, documentary filmmaker Ken Burns said Harris "embodies the possibilities that are America. Let us step back and embrace what this says about the promise of our country, the message it sends, especially to young people of all backgrounds."[59]

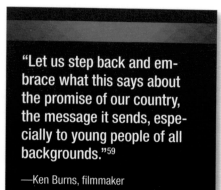

"Let us step back and embrace what this says about the promise of our country, the message it sends, especially to young people of all backgrounds."[59]

—Ken Burns, filmmaker

Though much of their campaigning was done online and through social media, Biden and Harris never stopped leading in the polls. They also raised much more money than Trump and Vice President Mike Pence. And while campaigns had to adjust to the health crisis, so too did the election process itself. Millions of Americans decided to vote by mail or drop off their ballots during early voting periods in the weeks prior to the November 3 election.

Remarkably, voting went rather smoothly, given the circumstances. However, because so many ballots were mailed in, counting the votes took longer than normal. So at the end of the night on November 3, there was no clear-cut winner. But

The First US Vice President of Color

Though Kamala Harris is the first woman of color to reach the office of vice president, she is not the first person of color to hold that office. That distinction belongs to Charles Curtis, who served as President Herbert Hoover's vice president from 1929 to 1933. Curtis was one-quarter Kaw Indian, and for much of his childhood he lived on the Kaw Nation reservation near Topeka, Kansas. Like Harris, Curtis was a prosecutor for several years before being elected to the Senate. Unlike Harris, Curtis was a Republican and served as the Senate's majority leader for four years before running for president in 1928. A vocal critic of Hoover and his policies, Curtis lost his bid to become his party's nominee for president. However, he agreed to accept the nomination as vice president, and together Hoover and Curtis won the White House in a landslide. Not shy about his roots, Curtis decorated his office in Washington, DC, with Native American art and artifacts. He and Hoover ran for reelection in 1932 but lost to Democrat Franklin Roosevelt and his running mate, John Nance Garner.

as the days went along and more areas of the country reported their voting tallies, it became clearer that the Biden-Harris ticket would prevail. Finally, on November 7, after it looked like Biden and Harris would take Pennsylvania, most media outlets called the race for the Democrats. Harris, out jogging, stopped to call Biden. "We did it, Joe. You're going to be the next president of the United States,"[60] Harris said before breaking into her trademark joyful laugh.

The final vote tally, announced four days after Election Day, was 306 electoral votes for Biden and Harris and 232 for Trump and Pence. After a month of recounts and audits, the popular vote became final with 81,281,502 votes for Biden and Harris and 74,222,593 votes for Trump and Pence. Both of those totals are higher than any other presidential ticket has ever received in a general election.

On the night of November 7, Harris joined Biden on an outdoor stage in Wilmington, Delaware, the city Biden has called home for most of his adult life. Before a raucous crowd braving the autumn chill, the winning candidates thanked their supporters and pledged to fulfill their many promises. Wearing a white pantsuit, in honor of the suffragists who spent years fighting for a woman's right to vote, Harris strode onstage and thanked Biden, the voters, and the campaign workers. And then she spoke about all of the women who made her victory possible—especially her mother:

When she came here from India at the age of 19 she maybe didn't quite imagine this moment. But she believed so deeply in an America where a moment like this is possible. So I am thinking about her and about the generations of women—Black women, Asian, white, Latina, Native American women—who throughout our nation's history have paved the way for this moment tonight. Women who fought and sacrificed so much for equality and liberty and justice for all.[61]

At her victory speech on November 7, 2020, Kamala Harris wore a white pantsuit as a way of honoring suffragists who had fought for women's voting rights.

The Inauguration

Trump never formally conceded the election. His supporters also refused to acknowledge the results. They protested around the country, citing Trump's baseless and unsubstantiated claims of vote fraud and abuse. Those claims culminated in a bloody riot on January 6, 2021, in the Capitol itself as Congress attempted to certify the election results. Although well aware of the threats swirling around them, Biden and Harris continued to build their new administration. On January 20, 2021, Joe Biden and Kamala Harris were officially sworn in as America's new president and vice president. Harris wore purple as a call for unity among "red" and "blue" state partisans and as an homage to pioneering Black politician Shirley Chisholm, who often wore the same color. On this momentous day, Harris stood before another pioneer, Supreme Court justice Sonia Sotomayor, the first Latina to serve on the Supreme Court. Harris placed her left hand on two Bibles held by Douglas Emhoff—one that had belonged to the late justice Thurgood Marshall and the other to Regina Shelton, a family friend from Oakland and a woman whom Harris often referred to as her "second mother." Standing nearby were Harris's sister, Maya, and Maya's daughter and granddaughters, as well as three former presidents and an array of distinguished guests. Harris raised her right hand and swore to defend the Constitution. The new president was sworn in next. Both stood ready to begin a new chapter in American history.

It was a historic day for many reasons. Harris had become the highest-ranking woman ever to serve in the US government. And while being first is remarkable, Harris has long maintained that the greater accomplishment is to make sure others will follow. Two years before she would make history alongside President Joe Biden, Harris delivered a speech to students at Spelman College, an HBCU in Atlanta, Georgia. She told them, "My mother would look at me and she'd say, 'Kamala, you may be the first to do many things, but make sure you are not the last.' That's why breaking those barriers is worth it. As much as anything else, it is also to create that path for those who will come after us."[62]

SOURCE NOTES

Introduction: The Groundbreaking Journey of Kamala Harris

1. Quoted in Paulina Jayne Isaac, "Kamala Harris Praises 'American Aspiration' in Her First Speech as Vice President," *Glamour*, January 21, 2021. www.glamour.com.
2. Quoted in Harshit Sabarwal, "Kamala Harris Recounts Childhood India Visits, Long Walks with Grandfather," *Hindustan Times* (New Delhi, India), August 16, 2020. www.hindustan times.com.
3. Quoted in Katherine J. Igoe, "Kamala Harris's Mom, Shyamala Gopalan, Inspires Kamala Every Day," *Marie Claire*, November 10, 2020. www.marieclaire.com.
4. Quoted in *Marie Claire*, "One of These Women Could Be Our Next President," February 21, 2019. www.marieclaire.com.

Chapter One: A Daughter of Immigrants

5. Quoted in Ellen Barry, "How Kamala Harris's Immigrant Parents Found a Home, and Each Other, in a Black Study Group," *New York Times*, September 13, 2020. www.nytimes.com.
6. Quoted in Barry, "How Kamala Harris's Immigrant Parents Found a Home, and Each Other, in a Black Study Group."
7. Quoted in Rev, "Joe Biden and Kamala Harris Speech Transcript August 12: First Campaign Event as Running Mates," August 12, 2020. www.rev.com.
8. Quoted in Natalie Orenstein, "Did Kamala Harris' Childhood in Berkeley Shape the Presidential Hopeful?," Berkeleyside, January 24, 2019. www.berkeleyside.com.
9. Quoted in Orenstein, "Did Kamala Harris' Childhood in Berkeley Shape the Presidential Hopeful?"
10. Quoted in Chirali Sharma, "Who Is Kamala Harris and Why Should India Know About Her?," Yahoo! News, August 13, 2020. https://in.news.yahoo.com.
11. Quoted in Igoe, "Kamala Harris's Mom, Shyamala Gopalan, Inspires Kamala Every Day."
12. Quoted in Daniel Dale, "U.S. Senator Kamala Harris's

Classmates From Her Canadian High School Cheer Her Potential Run for President," *Toronto Star*, December 29, 2018. www.thestar.com.

13. Quoted in David Shribman, "Kamala Harris: Montreal Embraces Its Onetime Daughter," *Los Angeles Times*, August 15, 2020. www.latimes.com.
14. Quoted in UC Hastings Law, "Toward Justice for All," 2013. www.uchastings.edu.

Chapter Two: Harris Finds Her Voice

15. Quoted in David Montgomery, "When Kamala Harris Helped Take Over a Howard University Building," *Washington Post*, April 30, 2019. www.washingtonpost.com.
16. Quoted in Montgomery, "When Kamala Harris Helped Take Over a Howard University Building."
17. Quoted in Montgomery, "When Kamala Harris Helped Take Over a Howard University Building."
18. Quoted in Tanya A. Christian, "HBCU Love: Kamala Harris Says Attending Howard Was a Childhood Dream," *Essence*, May 15, 2020. www.essence.com.
19. Quoted in Greg Rosalsky, "Where Kamala Harris Studied Economics," NPR, October 6, 2020. www.npr.org.
20. Quoted in Astead W. Herndon, "What Kamala Harris Learned About Power at Howard," *New York Times*, October 14, 2020. www.nytimes.com.
21. Quoted in Robin Givhan, "Kamala Harris Grew Up in a Mostly White World. Then She Went to a Black University in a Black City," *Washington Post*, September 16, 2019. www.washingtonpost.com.
22. Quoted in Montgomery, "When Kamala Harris Helped Take Over a Howard University Building."
23. Kamala Harris, *The Truths We Hold: An American Journey*. New York: Penguin, 2019.
24. Quoted in Elizabeth Weil, "Kamala Harris Takes Her Shot," *The Atlantic*, May 2019. www.theatlantic.com.
25. Quoted in Weil, "Kamala Harris Takes Her Shot."
26. Harris, *The Truths We Hold*.

Chapter Three: A Rising Star

27. Quoted in Christine Muschi, "How a Canadian Friend's Crisis Helped Shape Kamala Harris," *Toronto Globe and Mail*, January 19, 2021. www.theglobeandmail.com.
28. Quoted in Muschi, "How a Canadian Friend's Crisis Helped Shape Kamala Harris."

29. Quoted in Maeve Reston, "How Kamala Harris' Courtroom Experience Prepared Her for the Debate Stage," CNN, July 30, 2019. www.cnn.com.
30. Quoted in Justin Mendoza, "From the Archive: Here's a Look Back at Kamala Harris' Career as SF District Attorney, CA Attorney General," ABC7 News, November 7, 2020. https://abc7news.com.
31. Quoted in David Siders, "'Ruthless': How Kamala Harris Won Her First Race," *Politico*, January 24, 2019. www.politico.com.
32. Quoted in Siders, "'Ruthless.'"
33. Quoted in Mendoza, "From the Archive."
34. Quoted in Abby Aguire, "Kamala Harris Is Dreaming Big," *Vogue*, March 19, 2018. www.vogue.com.
35. Quoted in Andrea Wurzburger, "From a Blind Date to the White House: A Look at Kamala Harris and Doug Emhoff's Loving Relationship," *People*, January 21, 2021. https://people.com.
36. Quoted in Rachel McRady, "Kamala Harris and Doug Emhoff: Inside Their Relationship and Family Life," ET, January 20, 2021. www.etonline.com.
37. Quoted in Associated Press, "California Attorney General Kamala Harris Launches Bid for US Senate Seat," KPBS, January 13, 2015. www.kpbs.org.

Chapter Four: Senator Harris

38. Quoted in Iowa State University Archives of Women's Political Communication, "Victory Speech—November 8, 2016." https://awpc.cattcenter.iastate.edu.
39. Quoted in Julie Westfall, "'You Have the Power': California Sen. Kamala Harris Strikes a Defiant Tone at Women's March on Washington," *Allentown (PA) Morning Call*, January 21, 2017. www.mcall.com.
40. Quoted in Sean Cockerham, "Kamala Harris Introduces First Bill in the Senate, a Response to Trump Travel Ban," *Sacramento (CA) Bee*, February 9, 2017. www.sacbee.com.
41. Quoted in Aguire, "Kamala Harris Is Dreaming Big."
42. Quoted in Aguire, "Kamala Harris Is Dreaming Big."
43. Quoted in Aguire, "Kamala Harris Is Dreaming Big."
44. Quoted in Jessica Estepa, "Social Media Lights Up After Kamala Harris Questions Jeff Sessions," *USA Today*, June 13, 2017. www.usatoday.com.
45. Quoted in Jack Arnholz, "When Kamala Harris Took on Brett Kavanaugh and Bill Barr," ABC News, August 12, 2020. abcnews.go.com.
46. Quoted in Adam Edelman, "'We Have Zero Tolerance for Your Policy': Democrats Call on DHS' Nielsen to Resign," NBC News, June 19, 2018. www.nbcnews.com.

47. Quoted in Christina Wilkie, "Joe Biden Picks Sen. Kamala Harris to Be His Vice Presidential Running Mate, Making Her the First Black Woman on a Major Ticket," CNBC, August 11, 2020. www.cnbc.com.

Chapter Five: The Remarkable Path to the White House

48. Quoted in Scott Detrow, "Sen. Kamala Harris Announces 2020 Presidential Candidacy," NPR, January 21, 2019. www.npr.org.
49. Quoted in Jorge L. Ortiz, "'America, We Are Better than This': Kamala Harris Launches Presidential Campaign," *USA Today*, January 27, 2019. www.usatoday.com.
50. Quoted in Ortiz, "'America, We Are Better than This.'"
51. Quoted in Gene Demby, "Let's Talk About Kamala Harris," NPR, October 14, 2020. www.npr.org.
52. "Sen. Kamala Harris Announces 2020 Presidential Run," ABC News, January 21, 2019. https://abcnews.go.com.
53. Quoted in Jonathan Allen, "Kamala Harris, Joe Biden in Tense Exchange on Busing at Democratic Debate," NBC News, June 27, 2019. www.nbcnews.com.
54. Quoted in Armando Garcia, "Sen. Kamala Harris Suspends Presidential Bid," ABC News, December 3, 2019. https://abcnews.com.
55. Quoted in Joan Greve, "Kamala Harris: A Trailblazing 'Fearless Fighter for the Little Guy,'" *Irish Times* (Dublin, Ireland), August 12, 2020. www.irishtimes.com.
56. Quoted in Molly Ball and Charlotte Alter, "What Kamala Harris Means for Joe Biden's Campaign—and the Democratic Party's Future," *Time*, August 11, 2020. https://time.com.
57. Barack Obama (@BarackObama), "I've known Senator @Kamala Harris for a long time," Twitter, August 11, 2020, 5:16 p.m. https://twitter.com/barackobama/status/1293295296819220481?lang=en.
58. Quoted in Christina Wilkie, "Here's What Kamala Harris Said at the Democratic National Convention," CNBC, August 19, 2020. www.cnbc.com.
59. Quoted in Emily Glazer and Chad Day, "Kamala Harris Brings Hollywood Cash to Biden Campaign," *Wall Street Journal*, September 24, 2020. www.wsj.com.
60. "Kamala Harris Calls Joe Biden, 'We did it, Joe.'" CBS46, November 7, 2020. www.cbs46.com.
61. Quoted in Rhian Daly, "Kamala Harris Pays Tribute to Women Who 'Paved the Way' in History-Making Victory Speech," NME, November 8, 2020. www.nme.com.
62. Quoted in Spelman College, "U.S. Senator Kamala Harris Speaks at Spelman," October 26, 2018. www.spelman.edu.

IMPORTANT EVENTS IN THE LIFE OF KAMALA HARRIS

1964
Kamala Harris is born on October 20 in Oakland, California, to Shyamala Gopalan and Donald Harris.

1976
After her parents divorce, Harris moves with her mother and younger sister, Maya, to Montreal, where Gopalan takes a position as a professor and cancer researcher at McGill University.

1986
Harris graduates from Howard University with bachelor's degrees in economics and political science.

1989
Harris graduates from the University of California, Hastings College of the Law.

1990
Harris is admitted to the State Bar of California and becomes a deputy district attorney in Alameda County, California.

1998
Harris is hired as an assistant district attorney in San Francisco, eventually becoming chief of the Career Criminal Unit.

2000
Harris takes on a new role at San Francisco City Hall overseeing the Child and Family Services Division, which focuses on child abuse and neglect cases.

2003
Harris is elected district attorney of San Francisco, becoming the first person of color to be elected to that position. She is reelected in 2007.

2010
Harris wins her first statewide race when she is elected California attorney general. She is reelected in 2014.

2014
Harris and entertainment attorney Douglas Emhoff marry.

2016
With 62 percent of the vote, Harris defeats Representative Loretta Sanchez in the race for the US Senate.

2019
On January 21 Harris officially announces her candidacy for president of the United States; on December 3 she formally suspends her campaign.

2020
On August 11 Joe Biden announces Harris as his running mate; on November 3, US voters choose Biden and Harris as their new president and vice president.

2021
On January 20 Biden and Harris are officially sworn in as America's new president and vice president.

FOR FURTHER RESEARCH

Books

Peggy Brooks-Bertram and Arlette Miller Smith, *Dear Kamala: Women Write to the New Vice President*. Bloomington, IN: Red Lightning, 2021.

Shirley Chisholm, *Unbought and Unbossed*. Charlotte, NC: Take Root Media, 2010.

Kamala Harris, *The Truths We Hold: An American Journey*. New York: Penguin, 2019.

Dan Morain, *Kamala's Way: An American Life*. New York: Simon & Schuster, 2021.

Internet Sources

Melissa De Witte, "Breaking Barriers: Madame Vice President Kamala Harris," Stanford University, December 11, 2020. https://news.stanford.edu.

Editors of the L.A. Times, "Vice President Kamala Harris," *Los Angeles Times*, January 11, 2021. www.latimes.com.

Melissa Goldberg, "20 Kamala Harris Quotes That'll Inspire You to Take Charge," *Oprah Magazine*, January 20, 2021. www.oprahmag.com.

Alexis Okeowo, "Vice President Kamala Harris on the Road Ahead," *Vogue*, January 19, 2021. www.vogue.com.

Politico, "55 Things You Need to Know About Kamala Harris," www.politico.com.

Tessa Weinberg and Sruthi Palaniappan, "Kamala Harris: Everything You Need to Know About the New Vice President," ABC News, January 20, 2021. https://abcnews.go.com.

Websites

Ballotpedia: Kamala Harris (https://ballotpedia.org/Kamala _Harris). Ballotpedia tracks the political careers of Kamala Harris and other national figures, listing election results, committee assignments, key votes, and other news and information.

Howard University (www.howard.edu). Learn more about Kamala Harris's alma mater, Howard University, the oldest HBCU in the nation.

National Women's History Museum (NWHM) (www.womenshistory .org). The NWHM tells the story of women from all backgrounds who made their mark in American history, including Kamala Harris. The site has an online museum and plans to build a physical museum one day.

PolitiFact: Kamala Harris (www.politifact.com/personalities/kamala -harris). Sponsored by the Poynter Institute, PolitiFact investigates claims made by politicians and rates whether they are true or false or somewhere in between. The site is updated regularly. Learn how the statements made by Kamala Harris and other elected officials rank on the true/false scale.

United States Senate: President of the Senate: Vice President of the United States (www.senate.gov/reference/Index/Vice_President .htm). This website contains information about the duties of the vice president as explained in the Constitution, how the role has changed over time, and all of the people who have served in this important position.

White House: Kamala Harris (www.whitehouse.gov/administration /vice-president-harris). The official Biden-Harris administration profile of Kamala Harris includes photos and biographical information about the pioneering vice president.

INDEX

Note: Boldface page numbers indicate illustrations.

Adachi, Jeff, 23
Alameda County District Attorney's Office, 23–24, 25
Alpha Kappa Alpha (AKA) Sorority, 20, **22**, 23
Atlantic (magazine), 23

Back on Track program, 29
Barr, William, 39–40
Biden, Beau, 35
Biden, Joe
    declared winner by media, 51
    endorsement of Kamala Harris for Senate, 35
    first debate for presidential nomination, 45–46, **47**
    Kamala Harris chosen as running mate, 48
    on Kamala Harris's characteristics, 46–47
    sworn in as president, 53
    as unifier, 50
Black Baptist church, 12
Black Law Students Association (BLSA), 22–23
Boxer, Barbara, 34
Burns, Ken, 50

California attorney general
    criticism and defense of record, 32–33
    elections, 13, 31
    financial crisis beginning in 2008 and, 31–32
    for-profit colleges settlements for students, 32
    Open Justice online platform, 32
Chennai (formerly Madras), India, 5
Chisholm, Shirley, 53
civil rights movement (1960s), 6, 8–9
Clinton, Bill, 48
Clinton, Hillary, 32, 36, 50
coconut smashing, 13
Comey, James, 39
COVID-19, 47, 49
Cranston, Alan, 18, 34
Curtis, Charles, 51

dancing, 15
death penalty, 31
Deferred Action for Childhood Arrivals (DACA) program, 37–38

Eastland, James, 46
education
    Back on Track program, 29

of Gopalan, 8, 13
    Kamala Harris at middle and high schools, 15–16
    Kamala Harris's truancy program, 30
    of Maya Harris, 22, 32
    integration of schools, 10–12, 46
    See also Howard University, Washington, DC
Emhoff, Douglas (husband), **6**, **33**
    characteristics, 34
    Kamala Harris's swearing in as vice president, 53
    marriage, 34
environment, 28
Essence (magazine), 18, 23

family
    civil rights movement of 1960s and, 6
    father, 8–10, 19
    husband, **6**, **33**
        characteristics, 34
        Kamala Harris's swearing in as vice president, 53
        marriage, 34
    maternal grandfather, 5
    See also Gopalan, Shyamala (mother); Harris, Maya (sister)
Fazio, Bill, 28
Feinstein, Dianne, 31

Garcetti, Eric, 38
Garner, John Nance, 51
Good Morning America (television program), 44
Gopalan, Shyamala (mother), **11**
    characteristics, 13
    death, 6
    education, 8, 13
    Donald Harris and, 8–9
    Kamala Harris on
        being raised as confident Black woman, 14
        belief in America, 52
        characteristics of, 6
        importance of breaking barriers for others, 53
    Kamala Harris's campaign for San Francisco district attorney and, 28
    Kamala Harris's friend who was molested and, 25
    hometown, 5
    position at McGill University, 14
    University of California, Berkeley, and, 8–9, 16

Gore, Al, 48
Graham, Lindsey, 43
Green, Rodney, 18–19

Hallinan, Terrence, 27–28
Harris, Donald (father), 8–10, 19
Harris, Kamala Devi, **33**
    AKA and, 20, 23
    on Back on Track program, 29
    on ban on Muslims from entering US, 38
    on being of Black and Indian background, 13
    on Biden, 48
    characteristics
        ability to negotiate between different
            communities, 16
        activism, 14–15, 16, 17–18, 20–21, 22–23,
            46, 48
        ambition, 23
        charm, 23
        determination and strength, 7, 13, 43
        intelligence, 7, 43, 46
        as lawyer, 26
        poise, 15
        sense of humor, 7
    on Dreamers, 38
    education of, 11–12, 15–16
    as embodying possibilities of America, 50
    on Emhoff, 34
    father and, 9
    firsts accomplished by, 4–5, 29, 31, 35, 53
    on HBCUs, 21
    on importance of law and order for all
        communities, 45
    as key speaker at Women's March, 36
    on legal rights of migrant children, 37
    marriage, 34
    on maternal grandfather, 5
    Maya and
        childhood activism with, 14–15
        living with, 22
        presidential campaign, **14**
        swearing in as vice resident, 53
    meaning and pronunciation of name, 15
    on mother
        being raised as confident Black woman, 14
        belief in America, 52
        characteristics of, 6
        importance of breaking barriers for others, 53
    on participation in protests, 18
    on possibilities for all in US, 38–39
    on power of young women and girls, 7
    religion and, 12
    on school integration, 46
    on separation of migrant families, 43
    timeline of important events in life, 58–59
    on treating people's names with respect, 15
    vow to fight Trump agenda, 36
    on working for change as district attorney, 24
    See also Kamala Harris at under Howard
        University, Washington, DC
Harris, Maya (sister)
    career, 32

    childhood activism with Kamala, 14–15
    education, 22, 32
    father and, 9
    Kamala Harris living with, 22
    Kamala Harris's presidential campaign, **14**
    at Kamala Harris's swearing in as vice resident, 53
    marriage of Kamala Harris and Emhoff, 34
Hindu faith, 12–13
historically Black colleges and universities (HBCUs),
    21
Hoover, Herbert, 51
Howard University, Washington, DC, **19**
    basic facts about, 21
    Kamala Harris as first vice president who
        graduated from, 4
    Kamala Harris at
        as activist, 17–18, 20–21
        Alpha Kappa Alpha (AKA) Sorority and, 20
        decision to attend, 16
        inspiration from being among so many Blacks,
            18
        major areas of study, 19
        as public speaker, 19–20
        as student leader, 18–19
    Kamala Harris on importance of, 20
    Marshall at, 16

immigration
    DACA, 37–38
    Kamala Harris bill to guarantee legal access for
        people detained after arriving in US, 37
    Kamala Harris's beliefs about, 36
    Syrian refugee camp in Jordan, 38
    Trump ban on Muslims, 36–37
    Trump's separation of migrant children from
        parents, 41–43, **42**
Indian culture, 12–13
integration of schools, 10–12

Justice for Victims of Lynching Act (bill, 2018), 41

Kagan, Wanda, 25

legal profession and Kamala Harris
    Alameda County District Attorney's Office, 23–24,
        25
    characteristics as lawyer, 26
    decision to become lawyer, 16
    education, 21–23
    as head of the San Francisco City Attorney's Child
        and Family Services Division, 27
    Proposition 21, 26
    See also California attorney general; San Francisco
        District Attorney's Office
Lincoln Law School of San Jose, California, 32
Loftus, Suzy, 26
Los Angeles Times (newspaper), 16
lynching victims, 41

Madras (now Chennai), India, 5
Marie Claire (magazine), 7
Marshall, Thurgood, 16, 53

McGaffie, Sharon, 13
Midnight Magic dance troupe, 15
Miller, Stephen, 41
Montreal, Canada, 14–16
Motley, Constance Baker, 16

New York Times (newspaper), 9, 20
Nielsen, Kirstjen, 42–43
Now This (online news show), 34

Obama, Barack
    Biden as vice president under, 48
    endorsement of Kamala Harris for Senate, 35
    on Harris as vice presidential candidate, 49
Olioff, Paul, 15, 16
Open Justice online platform, 32

Paul, Rand, 41
Pelosi, Nancy, 31
Pence, Mike, 50
People (magazine), 15
Pink Ice Gala (AKA Sorority), in South Carolina, 20
Politico (magazine), 28–29
presidential election of 2016, 50
presidential election of 2020, **49**
    Biden and Harris as ticket of unity, 50
    COVID-19 and, 47, 49
    impeachment of Trump, 47
    polls, 50
    process of voting, 50
    results, 51
    Trump and supporters, 53
    See also presidential nomination campaign (2020);
      vice presidential campaign (2020)
presidential nomination campaign (2020), **14**
    AKA and, 20, **22**, 23
    announcement for, 44
    career as prosecutor and attorney general and, 45
    DACA, 38
    first debate for, 45–46, **47**
    as middle-ground candidate, 45
    as representative of the people, 44–45

recidivism, 29
Roosevelt, Franklin, 51
Rosario, Lita, 19–20
Rosenstein, Rod, 39

Sanchez, Loretta, 35
Sanders, Bernie, 45, 46, **47**
San Francisco City Attorney's Child and Family
    Services Division, 27
San Francisco District Attorney's Office
    as attorney in, 25–27
    campaign for district attorney, 27–29
    Hallinan as district attorney, 27
    Kamala Harris as district attorney, 29–31, **30**
    sworn in as district attorney, **11**
San Francisco Police Union, 31
segregation of schools, 10–12
Sessions, Jeff, 39, **40**
Shelton, Regina, 53
Sittenfeld, Tiernan, 28

Sotomayor, Sonia, 15, 53
South Asians for Biden, 5
Stanford Law School, 32

Talmadge, Herman, 46
Tamil language, 12–13
Thousand Oaks Elementary School, 11–12
Toronto Star (newspaper), 15
Trump, Donald, **40**
    election of 2016, 36
    election of 2020
      campaign, 47, 50
      failure to concede, 53
    firing of Comey, 39
    Kamala Harris's vow to fight agenda of, 36
    impeachment of (2020), 47
    separation of migrant children from parents,
      41–43, **42**
Truths We Hold: An American Journey, The (Kamala
    Harris), 11

University of California, Berkeley, 8–9, 16, 32
University of California, Hastings College of the Law,
    21–23
University of Wisconsin, Madison, 9
Upshaw, Karyn, 23
US Department of Homeland Security (DHS), 42–43
US Senate, Harris in
    bill to guarantee legal access for people detained
      after arriving in US, 37
    campaign for, 34, 35, **37**
    COVID relief, 41
    first trip as member, 38
    as intern for Senator Cranston, 18
    Justice for Victims of Lynching Act bill, 41
    removal of Miller, 41
    on Senate Intelligence Committee, 39–40
    separation of migrant children from parents,
      41–43, **42**
    as vice president, 48

vice presidency
    Curtis, 51
    duties of, 48
    Garner, 51
    Kamala Harris swearing in, 53
    issues pledging to focus on, 6
    oath taken, 4, 5, **6**
vice presidential campaign (2020)
    AKA and, 20, 23
    chosen by Biden, 48
    Kamala Harris as representative of the people,
      49
    Kamala Harris declared winner by media, 51
    Kamala Harris's victory speech, 51–52, **52**
Vogue (magazine), 38

Warren, Elizabeth, 31–32
Washington Post (newspaper), 17, 18, 20
Westmount High School, 15, 16
Whitfield, Gwendolyn, 17
Wilson, Frances, 12
Women's March, Washington, DC (2017), 36